Carnival

Grace Hallworth
Illustrated by Duncan Smith

CAMBRIDGE
UNIVERSITY PRESS

Cambridge Reading

General Editors

Richard Brown and Kate Ruttle

Consultant Editor

Jean Glasberg

PUBLISHED BY THE PRESS SYNDICATE OF THE UNIVERSITY OF CAMBRIDGE
The Pitt Building, Trumpington Street, Cambridge CB2 1RP, United Kingdom

CAMBRIDGE UNIVERSITY PRESS
The Edinburgh Building, Cambridge CB2 2RU, United Kingdom
40 West 20th Street, New York, NY 10011-4211, USA
10 Stamford Road, Oakleigh, Melbourne 3166, Australia

First published 1998
Reprinted 1998

Printed in the United Kingdom at the University Press, Cambridge

Typeset in Concorde

A catalogue record for this book is available from the British Library

ISBN 0 521 47703 4 paperback

**Other Cambridge Reading books
you may enjoy**

Garlunk
Helen Cresswell

Rachel's Mysterious Drawings
Richard Brown

A Walk with Granny
Nigel Gray

**Other books by Grace Hallworth
you may enjoy**

Cric Crac

Mouth Open Story Jump Out

A Web of Stories

1

"Georgie, it's time for bed."

"But Mammy, it's only eight o'clock! I'm not sleepy."

"Boy," said Pappy, "we have to be downtown by five o'clock tomorrow morning, or we'll miss the best part of Jouvay. Go to bed early and you'll get up on time."

Jouvay was the first day of Carnival. Bands of masqueraders would dance through the streets, with people crowding the sidewalks to watch.

This Jouvay, Georgie wanted to jump up with a big steel band. Once, when he was much younger, he and Mammy had danced with a band of masqueraders passing along their street. Just as he was beginning to enjoy the jump-up, Mammy pulled him onto the sidewalk. Long after the band turned the corner, he could hear the tune playing in his head, and he danced the steps he had seen Mammy dance. Now that he was older, he wanted to jump up in a big steel band.

Georgie's best friend Selwyn boasted that he was staying up all that night to jump up with Sun Valley Steel Band.

When Georgie told Pappy this, Pappy said, "The only place Selwyn will be jumping on Carnival Monday is in his bed. Selwyn's parents don't hold with Carnival."

As Georgie lay in bed that night, he heard Sun Valley boys in their pan yard playing one of his favourite calypsos. He sang the chorus softly. He didn't want Mammy to know he was still awake:

"One, two, three
Follow me . . ."

Georgie dreamt he was playing mas' in a King Sailor band. He wore a blue-and-white-striped T-shirt, blue denim trousers and a white sailor cap, and he was dancing the fireman dance to the music of steel pans. The masqueraders were on a stage that was bobbing up and down in the middle of the ocean. And people on land were waving and calling out:

"Play mas', Georgie,
Georgie boy, play mas'!"
Someone was singing:
"Georgie wake up boy, is Jouvay
And we must be on our way
Long before the break of day
Georgie wake up now!"
Georgie rubbed his eyes and sat up.

The dream faded out slowly like a film on television. Pappy was singing, and he and Mammy were dancing around Georgie's bed.

"Wake up, sleepy head! Rise and shine!" laughed Mammy.

2

Pappy was already dressed in a multicoloured shirt and black denim trousers. He wore his red cap with the peak at the back of his head.

Georgie leapt out of bed. "Pappy, you not going to leave me behind?"

"If you don't look sharp I might," said Pappy.

Mammy winked at Georgie. "Go and wash now," she said, "I already put your Carnival clothes out."

Georgie hurried to see what Mammy had chosen for him to wear.

"Wow!" he exclaimed. "Mammy, you didn't tell me!"

There was a pair of patchwork trousers, and a red shirt with a picture of midnight robbers in black.

Georgie showered quickly, hoping Mammy wouldn't waste time checking behind his ears and around his neck. He couldn't dry himself and put on his new clothes fast enough. Back in his bedroom, he pulled on his trainers and brushed his hair.

"Oui Pappa! Who is this sharp-looking dude?" teased Pappy when Georgie rushed into the kitchen.

"Pappy! I hear a band coming – it's time to go!"

"It's all right, Georgie. There'll be lots of bands passing. You sit down and eat your breakfast."

Georgie was so excited he hardly touched the sandwiches Mammy had made for him. Before he and Pappy left, Mammy slipped some money in his shirt pocket and zipped it up. "You're sure to get hungry. Buy yourself something to eat – no sweets mind!"

3

It was just gone four in the morning when they set out, but it looked like the middle of the night. A pale moon broke up the darkness below. Here and there in the shadows were the shapes of people waiting. Georgie and Pappy stood with a group dressed in old, ragged clothes – Old Mas' costumes – waiting to join a band and dance their way to the square downtown. There, they'd see King Carnival open the festival.

"Mas' comin'!" someone called out, and Georgie felt a shiver of excitement.

There were five of them. Out of the darkness, Georgie saw a creature with eyes as red as live coals, and a row of pointed black horns standing out across his forehead. It was a Jab Moulassie – a

Molasses Devil – with chains around his ankles and wrists, a long, scaly tail, and his body caked with grime. The others were his imps – dressed in red from top to toe. When they danced, their tails seemed to writhe and rear up like angry snakes.

The imps pointed their long wooden forks at people as they danced around them chanting,

"Jab Moulassie
Jab Moulassie
Jab Moulassie, Jab . . ."

Georgie held Pappy's hand tightly.

"Don't look scared," Pappy whispered to Georgie. "If you do they'll smear grease and dirt all over your clothes. They want to make everybody dirty like them."

Georgie closed his eyes – maybe if he couldn't see them, he wouldn't be frightened. But he knew they were coming closer.

He heard Pappy say, "What kinda dance is that, man? Let me show you how to do a real devil dance!"

Georgie opened his eyes. He couldn't believe it! There was Pappy dancing with the devil and his imps, laughing, leading them away from him.

The dancing was interrupted by the sound of music coming from a side-street. It was another band and people ran to join it.

The devil called out, "Mr Dancer, I'll catch you downtown," and he and his imps ran off with the others. Georgie shuddered at the thought of meeting them again. And yet, he thought he knew that voice.

"Pappy, you think we could join a band?" Georgie asked anxiously.

"Of course!" said Pappy. "Jumping up in a band is the best way to travel and feel no pain. But we will wait for a *steel* band."

4

They didn't have long to wait.

In the distance they heard the ping-pong of a steel band and the shushing sound of feet shuffling in time to a rhythm. As the band drew near, Georgie read the name on the banner held high by two girls at the front.

"Pappy, it's Sun Valley!" he exclaimed.

"Georgie, stay close to me," Pappy warned. "Don't let me out of your sight. If I lose you today, your mother will never let me forget it."

Georgie and Pappy were soon close to the drummers. The sound of bass drums filled the street:

Bidim boom bididim boom.
Bodoodoom bodoodoom bididim boom . . .
     The vibrations echoed inside Georgie's
head and he felt them booming against his
chest. Ripples of sound ran down his legs

until they reached the soles of his feet and made him jump higher and higher as he sang,

"One, two, three
Follow me . . ."

Pappy was dancing and singing too.

Sun Valley's followers spread out to the very edges of the street to give themselves room to dance, to jump, to wave their arms in time with the rhythm of the drums. People on the sidewalks swayed. Some of them were drawn into the band almost against their will.

Georgie danced and sang in his midnight robber clothes. He looked around at all the other extraordinary costumes. Someone disguised as a brown bat was dancing with a donkey. Georgie'd never seen a Donkey mas' before and was just moving over to have a closer look when he was roughly pushed forward. A group of boys charged through the band, thrusting people aside, then ran away.

Georgie tried to work his way back to where he thought Pappy was, but he couldn't see him anywhere. He noticed that, although people were dancing, they weren't moving forward. The band had come to a crossroads, and bands were pouring in from all directions. The Sun Valley band was surrounded, its followers pressed closely together.

Georgie, who was trapped in the middle of the band, felt as though all the breath was being squeezed out of him.

He had to get some air. He began weaving his way through the crowd, but suddenly a hand clasped his wrist and held him fast.

"What's your hurry, little Georgie? If you seek death, I am he!"

The ghostly voice came from behind the grinning mask of a skull head. It was partly covered with the black hood of a black cape. Under the cape was a skeleton holding a scythe. Georgie, terrified by the spectre, wrenched his hand from the skeleton's bony grasp, and fled.

5

At last, Georgie found a place where he could breathe more easily. But the crowd moved like a flood sweeping everything along in its path. Georgie found himself swept into the midst of a band of clowns dancing to the music of guitars and mandolins. Their faces were painted chalky white, and they had scarlet mouths, brightly coloured wigs and red noses.

Georgie looked at the faces in the crowd, hoping he'd see Pappy. Instead, he caught sight again of the Brown Bat. The bat wasn't wearing his mask – he looked a little lost, and Georgie plucked up courage to go and talk to him.

"I saw you in Sun Valley. But where is the Donkey mas' that was with you?" he asked.

"We were separated in the confusion back there."

"I lost my dad," said Georgie. "I don't know where he is."

"Well, Sun Valley was heading for the Square. Maybe you'll find him there. Look," he added, seeing Georgie's worried face, "I'm going to meet my band at the Quay. I'll walk you to the Square."

When they got to the Square, the Bat said, "I'm sure you'll find your dad around here somewhere. When you do, look out for our band – it's called Old Time Mas'. We'll be heading back to the Western Main Road."

6

Georgie found a place to stand, but it was so far back from the road he couldn't see the bands passing. He heard the sound of clapping and a voice making an announcement. It was coming from the Carnival Stand nearby. Georgie realised it was probably King Carnival opening the festival – and he was missing it all. But at that moment, all he really wanted was to find Pappy. He imagined Pappy returning home without him. Mammy would cry and she would be so vexed with Pappy she wouldn't talk to him for days. Pappy's own parents would be angry too when they heard what had happened. Everyone would be so sad they wouldn't want to go out in the afternoon and see the parade of bands in their fantastic costumes. "And it will all be *my* fault," thought Georgie. Tears filled his eyes and rolled down his cheeks.

"Hey, Georgie! Hey!"

Georgie quickly brushed the tears away and looked around.

"Up here – in the tree!"

He looked up. There was someone sitting way up high in one of the trees. Georgie couldn't see who it was.

"It's ME, Selwyn!" Georgie couldn't believe it. What was Selwyn *doing* all the way up there?

"You here by yo'self?" Selwyn shouted. He sounded just as surprised to see Georgie.

"Selwyn, you see Pappy anywhere? I was with him in Sun Valley band."

"Boy, you lose yo' father? You'll *never* find him here today!" But Selwyn saw that his friend was in a bad fix. "Listen on, Georgie. Sun Valley come and gone long time. Why don't you stay here for a while and see some mas'. Then we can go home!"

But Georgie had started to panic.

"No!" he shouted. "I *have* to find Pappy!" He turned to go – though with no idea where to start looking.

"Wait, Georgie!" called Selwyn. "I comin' with you!"

At that moment, there was a loud crack and a terrified scream. Selwyn's sudden movement had caused the branch to split, so that it was hanging down with Selwyn clinging on to it, still high above the ground.

"Georgie! Help me! HELP! HELP!"

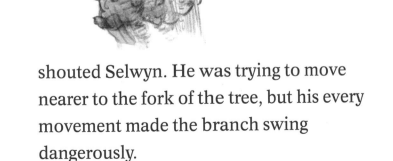

shouted Selwyn. He was trying to move
nearer to the fork of the tree, but his every
movement made the branch swing
dangerously.

"Oh Lord! Somebody help me! HELP!
I go fall!"

7

Georgie didn't know what to do. He felt helpless – what could he *do*? Just across the road from the Square, he saw two Moko Jumbies and a third one being helped down from his stilts. This gave Georgie an idea – perhaps the Moko Jumbies could help!

"Selwyn," he called. "Hold on! I'll go and get help."

Georgie ran as fast as he could to where the Moko Jumbies were standing. He grabbed hold of the one who'd just come off his stilts.

"Mister!" he said. "Please come and help my friend. He's up in the tree and can't get down."

"Hold on, boy," said the man. "Tell me slowly. What's the trouble?"

"It's my friend
Selwyn. He's on a
branch high high up.
But it crack and it
swinging and . . ."
Georgie didn't have
any breath left to go on.

The man called up
to the two others on
their stilts. "Come on
fellas, we got an
emergency here."

Georgie and the
man set off running
across the grass. The
two Moko Jumbies,

tall as trees, came stomping along the paved pathway. A large crowd had gathered around the tree. People were calling out, telling Selwyn what he should or should not do. The boy was silent.

"George Sampson! So we meet again!" Georgie whirled round to see the dreaded skeleton standing right next to him. This time, though, Georgie recognised the voice as that of his teacher, Mr Williams. The teacher removed his frightening skull mask. "What's happening here, boy?"

"It's Selwyn, sir. He's up there on the branch. An' it breaking up!"

Meanwhile, the two Moko Jumbies had caught up with their friend, who was testing the firmness of the ground around the tree.

"The earth kinda soft with the rain we been having," said the friend. "If we could find something hard to put over the grass!"

Georgie remembered that Pappy had once put a flattened cardboard box under his car wheels when they were spinning on a muddy road.

"Sir," he said to Mr Williams, "what about some cardboard boxes? We could flatten them and spread them out."

"Good idea, George! But where would we find the boxes?"

"They should have plenty empty boxes in the Stand with all the bottled drinks they sellin'," said one of the Moko Jumbies. At once, the Moko Jumbies' friend sprinted across to the Carnival Stand.

Georgie could hardly bear to look up at Selwyn, who was so high up he couldn't see his face. But he could hear his friend's soft crying, and he could feel his fear. Georgie thought of Selwyn falling from the branch and breaking his leg, perhaps even dying. Mr Williams put his hand on Georgie's shoulder. "It will be all right, George. We'll get him down.

8

The cardboard boxes were flattened and spread out over the grass. The Moko Jumbies stepped from the path onto the cardboard matting. One of them brushed against the branch and it swayed slightly. There was a gasp from the crowd. Georgie heard Selwyn cry out and he held his breath.

"Easy, boy!" said one of the Moko Jumbies.

Their friend was climbing the tree in case he needed to lend a hand. It was just as well – Selwyn's feet were numb and he couldn't stand. The Moko Jumbies moved Selwyn along the branch until they were able to place him on their friend's back – the boy was brought down piggy-back, his arms tightly clasped around the man's neck.

The crowd cheered the Moko Jumbies. Selwyn told them he would never forget them, and promised them he would never climb such a tall tree ever again. Some of the crowd followed the Moko Jumbies as they left, dancing and singing all the way through the Square. Others began to drift back to watch the parade of bands.

Mr Williams rubbed the soles of Selwyn's feet until he was able to stand and they set off, slowly. But suddenly, *Georgie's* legs felt shaky.

"Sir, I feelin' faint," he whispered.

"All right, let's sit here and take a rest," said Mr Williams.

They all sat on the cool grass.

"What we need after all that excitement is something to fill that hollow feeling, eh boys?"

Georgie nodded half-heartedly. He knew the hollow feeling wouldn't go away until he found his father. He told

Mr Williams all that had happened that morning.

"Don't worry, George. I'll take you both home if we don't find your father. But I'm sure he's still around here looking for you. Let's go to the Quay for some food."

Georgie felt a rush of relief – Mr Williams would make everything right again.

9

The two boys and their teacher walked
across the Square to the Quay, a broad
street that led to the docks. On the Quay,
Georgie saw stalls selling all kinds of food.
He heard the crackle of corn-on-the-cob
roasting on grids over coal-pot fires, the
sizzle of black pudding frying. Smells

mingled – codfish-in-batter, hot hops loaves – making Georgie's mouth water and his stomach heave with hunger.

Georgie wanted to stop right here and buy something, but Mr Williams and Selwyn walked on. Mr Williams was heading for a stall that was well away from the hustle and bustle of the stalls in the centre of the Quay. In charge of the stall was an old lady, so small she looked like a child. But when she spoke, her voice was deep and strong.

"Aie! Aie! Sunny, is you? How you do?" she greeted Mr Williams.

"I doing fine, Ma Landeau. How you going?" They hugged each other.

"As you see, son. As you see. Tell me, who are your little friends?"

"Ah!" said Mr Williams. "These are two of my pupils. And Georgie here just saved his friend from falling out of a tree. I've brought them for some of your famous

corn soup."

"If you can wait about five minutes, you'll have a fresh brew of corn soup," she promised.

"Fine. You two boys wait here with Ma Landeau – I'm just going to dash down the road to the store and get something for my costume. I'll be back soon."

As soon as Mr Williams had gone, Selwyn, too hungry to wait, said to

Georgie, "I just going over there to get a roast corn," and went off towards a nearby stall.

Georgie waited for his soup.

"I know Sunny since he was a little boy, younger than you," said Ma Landeau. "Now he is a big teacher. Imagine that, eh! Tell me, he teach you good?"

Georgie said he was the best teacher in the whole school, and he was good at football too. Then, before he knew it, he found himself telling the old lady about losing his Pappy.

"Your Mammy didn't come with you?" she asked, full of concern.

"No. Mammy don't like Carnival too much. She prefer to look at it on television. Besides, she like to stay at home and prepare for all the family coming to stay."

"You have a big family then?"

"Yes. Mammy's brother and his whole family coming to spend two days. And Pappy will go and bring his mom and dad in the car. They live here in the city but they spend some time at our house too. Maybe they will take us to see pretty mas' in the afternoon."

"My grandson collect things from the pretty mas' bands every year . . ."

But Georgie wasn't listening any more. He was looking around wildly. He could hear a familiar drumming. It was the same kind of drumming he had heard earlier that morning.

"What's the matter?" asked Ma Landeau.

"I think I hear the devils coming!" He
had to find a place to hide. There was a
tent at the back of the stall – he rushed
into it and pulled the curtains to close up
the opening. And not a moment too soon.
The next second, the devils arrived.

10

The devils surrounded the old lady, chanting.

"Food! Food! Hot food!

Time for food! Hot food!"

Georgie heard a voice say, "Boy, I so hungry I could eat a horse!"

He couldn't stop shaking. If the devil could eat a horse, what chance was there for him, a small boy! If only Mr Williams would come back. He peeped through a gap in the curtains and saw an ugly scaly beast squirming on the grass.

"Down, hell-hound! Crawl on your belly, you miserable worm. Eat the dust!" An imp was cracking a whip.

Georgie quickly pulled the curtains together again and looked around the tent.

The walls were covered with fantastic masks, headpieces and banners. High in the corner, Georgie saw a fearsome dragon mask – he couldn't take his eyes from it.

The mask was made of beaded pearls, and sunk deep into blackened holes was a pair of glittering eyes. Georgie felt those eyes staring at him and looked away at the white pointed fangs that stuck out of the dragon's bright red gaping mouth. A mass of green snake-like coils and white spikes was attached to the mask. In the half-light of the tent, the mask looked like a real face, alive and full of anger.

Georgie shivered and moved as far back from the mask as he could.

Suddenly, Georgie heard the old lady cry out, "All you stop yo' skylarking! I too old for this dancing and excitement."

The drumming was getting faster and louder. He peeped out again. Two devils were dancing the old lady round and

round. The imps were jumping about and
singing,

"Going down with a bunch of roses
Going down
We go take you below
Going down with a bunch of roses
Going down
Where the fires glow
Going down . . ."

He was sure they were the same band that Pappy had danced with, but there seemed to be more of them.

The old lady was trying to free herself from the devils but they held on to her arms and would not let her go.

Whatever happened, Georgie knew he had to do something to help her. But these were real devils! They had long pointed horns that seemed to come from inside their heads. They ate horses for breakfast, and had a beast so fierce that it was kept on a chain.

But when Georgie heard them laughing at the old lady, he grew so angry he forgot to be afraid. His eyes were drawn back to the dragon mask. The dragon's eyes seemed to share the anger he felt. Without thinking, Georgie climbed on a chair, took down the mask and put it over his head and face. The green coils covered his head and the sides of his face, and came down

to his neck. Georgie grabbed the wooden
sword which hung from a hook, and
rushed out of the tent. But in his haste, he
forgot to pull the curtains aside. They
came loose and wrapped themselves
around him, tripping him up and pitching
him headlong into the group of dancing
devils and imps.

As they all fell, they knocked over the saucepan of corn soup. Some of the hot liquid spilled on the beast who leapt up and cried out, "Jeez an' ages! All yo' go set me on fire, oui! Just stop this bassa-bassa, yo' cunumunu idiots!" He was standing upright now, and clouted one of the imps who began to wail loudly. The other imps hurled names at the beast as though they were pelting stones at an attacking dog.

"Rat's teeth!" one shouted.

"Yeah! Get off, dog's breath!" added another.

11

The uproar brought a crowd of people to
the scene, Mr Williams among them.

The old lady was giving the devils and
imps a piece of her mind.

"All yo' boys better forget playin' mas'
this morning, and put yo' minds to
cleaning up this mess you make here."

Someone was unwrapping the
drapes from around Georgie.

"Pappy! I knew Mr Williams would find you!" cried Georgie. Pappy was hugging him and trying to be cross at the same time.

"Georgie, what *are* you up to?"

"Pappy, I was trying to stop the devils from taking Ma Landeau down below." He turned to the old lady. "I wanted to frighten them away. I didn't mean to cause any trouble," he finished tearfully.

"I'm not mad at you, dearie." Then she spoke to Pappy. "Don't you scold him neither. He's a brave boy to face those mad devils." She glared at the imps, and Georgie realised for the first time what young boys they were – just boys, pretending to be devils and devils' imps.

Pappy laughed and said, "Well, it seems as though Georgie has done nothing but rescue people all morning!"

He went across to one of the devils and led him to Georgie.

"Now Georgie, do you know who this is?"

Georgie looked very carefully. His eyes lit up – it was his good friend and next-door neighbour, Mr Ali. "Ooooh! It's Mr Ali! When I heard the voice this morning, I *knew* I'd heard it before!" said Georgie.

"Well, Georgie, I fooled you," said Mr Ali, "but you *terrified* me when you rushed out in that dragon mas' boy!" Georgie could tell Mr Ali was teasing.

12

The imps had been sent off by the old lady to fetch water for her corn soup, and Mr Ali gave her some money to make up for the soup that had been spilled. She gave the dragon mask to Georgie. "Now you can start your own Carnival collection," she said.

Ma Landeau put on another pan of corn soup. It was going to be a special brew, she said. And when they drank it, everyone agreed that they had never tasted soup like it. "Not even down below!" added the beast.

They were just about to leave when Selwyn rushed up. "Sir, Sir! I just see a band up the Quay. Is a music band and they going along the Western Main Road." Everyone ran to the top of the Quay.

Georgie saw a banner that read, Old Time Mas'.

"Pappy!" he cried. "It's my friend's band."

A familiar voice said, "Hi pal! So you found your father?" It was the Brown Bat. "Look, I found my donkey friend too." The Donkey mas' took off her headpiece to say hello.

Georgie put on his dragon mask. Selwyn had no costume so the donkey lent him her headpiece. Then the boys, Pappy, Mr Williams, Mr Ali and his devils and imps all joined the band of Old Mas' characters.

Georgie was going to enjoy this jump-up back home with Pappy. Who knows, the band might even pass in front of their house. Then Mammy, his cousins and all the neighbours would see him playing Old Mas'!

The band broke into Georgie's favourite calypso,
"One, two, three
Follow me . . ."